MW01154091

Food Truck Empire Presents:

How to Build Your Own Food Truck

A Guide to Converting a Used Truck into a Profitable Mobile Food Unit From Four People That Have Done it.

How to Build Your Own Food Truck

A Guide to Converting a Used Truck into a Profitable Mobile Food Unit From Four People That Have Done it.

Copyright © 2015 Food Truck Empire

http://www.foodtruckempire.com

ISBN-13: 978-0-9899527-2-9

Published by JPM Publishing

Wisconsin, USA

All Rights Reserved

Publisher's note

This book is part of the Food Truck Empire family. Included with your purchase are several interviews available for download in .mp3 format. The links to download these interviews are listen on this page, and again on the page in which details of each interview are contained.

Interview 1:
http://foodtruckempire.libsyn.com/episode-034-interview-with-bob-pierson

Interview 2:
http://traffic.libsyn.com/foodtruckempire/Episode_049_-_final.mp3

Interview 3:   http://foodtruckempire.libsyn.com/the-boiler-monkey-interview

Interview 4: http://foodtruckempire.libsyn.com/episode-018-interview-with-mark-s-grill-and-how-to-handle-bad-reviews

PART ONE

WHAT YOU NEED TO KNOW

What You Need to Know Before Purchasing a Food Truck

This might seem obvious, but we see people making this mistake over and over again. Folks find an old bread truck, BBQ trailer or other (potentially) operational vehicle that's a "great" deal. They want to snatch up this opportunity while it's still available to avoid missing out on their one chance to buy a truck.

This is understandable because finding a quality used trucks that's been correctly cared for can be a challenge at times. However, this is not the right way to approach finding a vehicle for your future mobile food business. These are the things you need to get straightened out before you make a purchase.

Figure out What Type of Truck You Need

Before you even start to look for a vehicle, you need to figure out what type of food you're going to be serving on your truck. Why is this so important? Because the type of food you serve will dictate the type of equipment you'll need to install on the vehicle. If you're planning to start an ice cream truck, you'll have an entirely different set of equipment needs than if you start a taco truck.

Here's the process we recommend taking to ensure you've got the right amount of space on your truck to operate a business. Fortunately, this important step isn't complicated. It only requires taking the time to write down what you need and figuring out how much space each piece of equipment will require.

Refrigerator – 3 feet wide, 7 feet high

Deep Fryer – 4 feet wide, 4 feet high

Prep Station – 4 feet wide, 4 feet high

Note: For each piece of equipment you plan to install on your truck, make sure you list exactly how much space it will take up in the truck. This includes the height of the equipment in the vehicle. In some instances, first time food truck builders have mistakenly purchased trucks with cabins that are too low in height to fit in their cabinets and refrigerators. Don't make this rookie mistake!

Equipment Space: You should always build in a little wiggle room when planning how to load cooking equipment into a truck. You'll need space to walk around in the vehicle. Best case scenario, you may want to leave some open space to be able to add additional items later. If you decide to expand into serving coffee or ice cream as an up-sell later, you'll need room to for it. Even if it's going to be used for nothing more than storage, you will be glad you didn't max out your space immediately.

Pro Tip: Don't forget to add space for safety items like a fire extinguisher. Not only will this help keep you and your future employees safe, you'll need to have this on board to be able to operate legally in most locations.

Open Space: You're going to be spending a lot of hours in the cabin of your truck so don't forget to leave space to walk around the cabin. You'll want additional space if you plan to work with another individual in the truck. One clever way to get a sense of how much space will be available in the truck is to get a map out what the inside of the truck would be like on your driveway or garage using chalk. This is a quick way you can get sense of the space that would be left in the vehicle after loading in the equipment.

Average Truck Sizes: A standard size of a food truck has a 16" – 18" cabin. Typically, you want a ceiling that is at least 7 feet high within the cabin so that you can comfortably walk around the space and support larger appliances like refrigerators and even overhead cabinets in certain cases.

Check with Your City for Special Regulations: Different cities have unique and changing laws when it comes to letting food trucks operate in their city. Before you buy your food truck, make sure you understand what these special requirements are. In larger cities, there are often restrictions on the size of food truck you can operate legally. Without having this knowledge you could end up buying a truck that has no way of being operated legally… a costly overlook.

You will need to contact the city you live in to identify what's required in your area. You can also ask a friendly food truck that operates locally for advice. All food truckers will have gone through this process and can save you hours of calls into your local government offices for more information.

Some of the requirements of food trucks just about everywhere are as follows:

- You need a fire extinguisher on board.
- You need an overhead duct to release heat from a grill.
- You need a 3 compartment sink to allow workers to wash their hands. You'll also need a soap dispenser and water tank that will take in the waste.
- You'll need hot water on board.

After you understand the equipment needed on the truck and the regulations of the city, you will be able to determine what size of a food truck to purchase.

As you'll learn from the audio interviews included in this book, building a food truck for the first time will be an extremely frustrating experience. On more than one occasion, you'll wonder why a certain piece of equipment isn't working correctly. Getting the electrical wiring built into the truck could be one of those challenging moments. Be mentally prepared for this. If you want to build a food truck, you can do it, but it will take some time if it's your first experience building something so complex.

As a general rule of thumb, be prepared to be building your truck for around 2 – 3 months to work out the problems. Be prepared to invest a few thousand dollars past your initial estimates to get the vehicle up to code. Bottom line, it always costs more to build a food truck than you think it will at first.

The plus side of going through this process is that at

the end of the day you'll have an in-depth understanding of how your food truck works. This knowledge will be invaluable as you launch your business and begin operating your food truck full-time. When you know exactly how your truck works, inside and out, you will also know how to fix the vehicle. This will help save money in repairs and ultimately cut expenses for the business. Who knows... You might even be able to setup a side hustle fixing other people's food trucks once the local vendors get to know you.

PART TWO

INTERVIEWS

What to Look For in a Used Food Truck

Download This MP3 Interview Here:

http://foodtruckempire.libsyn.com/episode-034-interview-with-bob-pierson

Bob Pierson is the owner of M&R Trailers. M&R has built concession vehicles for over 5 years and he has a wealth of experience finding and evaluating used food trucks. I found out about Pierson through the large collection of YouTube videos (links to videos below) he's produced demonstrating how to build a truck.

In this discussion, Pierson shares his tips for finding quality used trucks and his advice on evaluating whether or not a vehicle will operate longterm. Don't invest in a truck before listening to this interview!

- Why you should consider purchasing a used truck from a business fleet first. Think bread trucks, UPS, FedEx, and other related companies. These businesses have strict maintenance policies in place so you can be more confident they've been treated well.

- Bring a mechanic to help evaluate any truck prior to purchase. This can go a long way to ensuring you won't end up with a lemon. Don't buy on the word of the dealer.

- Why Pierson approaches building a food truck similar to the way he would a construction site

- Pierson doesn't recommend purchasing a truck that has less than a 7 foot high ceiling. It can be difficult to get cooking equipment into the truck if you get lower than that.

- Why you should have an understanding of how

much room you need prior to looking for a truck. Figure out how much room you need first... Then start looking for a truck that fits your needs.

- Some of the common sense things you should take into account before you buy a used food truck, including trying to estimate the cost of improvements, upgrades, or changes you'll need to make on the vehicle.

- Why you'll need electrical, gas, plumbing, welding, and framing skills to build an operational food truck.

- Why it's often easier and cheaper to hire out a professional to convert a truck instead of trying to do it yourself.

- Why M&R Concessions recommends Cummings Onan generators versus cheaper variations

- The common mistakes that are made when building or converting a food truck

- The importance of getting a truck built up to health code requirements. In the coming years, Pierson expects regulations to tighten in this area.

Resources

M&R Trailers (http://www.mr-concessions.com/) – This is Bob Pierson's business. They've been building food trucks more than 5 years and are located in Macclenny, Florida.

How to Build a Concession Truck

(http://youtu.be/3yclUd9EMZA)– In this 12-minute video, Pierson walks provides a high-level overview of a gutted truck before the cooking equipment has been added to a truck and explains the work that will be done in the future. After outlining the framing process where equipment including the generator will be located, you also get fast forwarded and get to see the final product. This is a truck that was built for a customer.

DIY Food Truck Design and Build Out

Download This MP3 Interview Here:

http://traffic.libsyn.com/foodtruckempire/Episode_049
_-_final.mp3

Just like building a house. You can't just build a house from an idea in your head. You need a blue print. - **Jeremy Campeau on designing a food truck**

Jeremy Campeau designed and built a food truck with no previous experience for somewhere between $20,000 – $30,000. Sure, there were some speed bumps along the way and a lot of troubleshooting needed, but the final product speaks for itself with Buffy's Mexi-Casian Grill (https://www.facebook.com/MexiCasianGrill) now roaming the streets of Lincoln Park, MI. If you're in the process of designing or ever thought about building a food truck of your own, you won't want to miss this episode of the program.

Campeau has been a life-long entrepreneur. In his teens he started a repair shop and now own his own successful construction business. But it was a cousin's layoff from her job that pulled him into building a food truck. Jeremy's cousin had recently been laid off from her job and was ready to go into business for herself. That's when the idea of building a the food truck first formed.

In this interview, Campeau shares what the process was like for him to build his first truck. This includes everything from how they found a used bakery truck, to shopping around for deeply discounted used cooking equipment at local auctions to get the best deal and ultimately install their equipment. Jeremy also highlights the importance of having a clear understanding of what your menu will be prior to beginning the design phase.

Stuff You'll Learn in the Audio Interview

- Why a bakery truck was selected as the foundation of the food truck

- How Jeremy Campeau designed the interior layout of their concession truck

- Some of the mistakes that were made while building Buffy's Mexi-Casian Grill

- Why Jeremy worked with an architect to determine where to install cooking equipment in the truck

- How to find out about auction sales and restaurant closures where cooking equipment may be sold

- How they purchased a serving window at Lowe's that can more easily fit into a truck.

- Why Jeremy wanted to truck to be in line with commercial kitchen code

- The reasons you should consult with a professional electrician even if you plan on building a truck yourself.

- The length of time it took to design and build the vehicle from start to finish.

Quote from The Show

*If you're going to get into this it's time and money. It's a huge cost of time and money so you really want to either hire experts or you want to plan a lot and research a lot. – **Jeremy Campeau on what you should do if you're thinking about building a food truck.***

Resources

Buffy's Mexi-Casian Food Truck (https://www.facebook.com/MexiCasianGrill)- This is the food truck referenced during the show. They serve up Mexi-American fusion food to the hungry residents of

Lincoln Park, Michigan, located close to Detroit. Check them out if you live in the area.

Harbor Freight (http://www.harborfreight.com/)- This is the store Jeremy Campeau goes to purchase the tools needed to customize his food truck. This is the ideal place to find things like metal sheers or grinding wheels.

Auction Zip

(http://www.auctionzip.com/restaurantequipment.html)- Use this website to help find auctions near you that are discounted restaurant equipment. This is a terrific way to save money on mobile kitchen supplies.

How to Build a Food Truck Yourself (http://foodtruckempire.com/how-to/build-a-food-truck/)- A more in-depth, step by step article on building a food truck.

You don't need to build a food truck. Matt built a food bus.

Download This MP3 Interview Here:

http://foodtruckempire.libsyn.com/the-boiler-monkey-interview

Matt Fuemmeler went on a trip with his wife to South America and came back determined to start a food truck. After returning state side and doing more research Fuemmeler decided that he wanted something a little bit different than the traditional style truck. Eventually, he stumbled upon a vintage bus he discovered on eBay that fit his concept so he called the owner and decided to pull the trigger. Fuemmeler bought an airplane ticket from Albuquerque, New Mexico, to Seattle, Wash., and the plan was to drive the bus back home. But the journey wouldn't go that smoothly.

On the trip home Fuemmeler's bus would break down in Portland during rush hour... resulting in some coverage from the local news as he vehicle held up traffic. Later, he would experience tire problems in Needles, Calif., that would also slow him down. But eventually, Fuemmeler got his bus back to New Mexico where he and his brother begin the 3-month process of converting the bus into a bustaurant.

Stuff You'll Learn

- How Fuemmeler learned to cook crepes by working as an employee at another food cart

- How Fuemmeler almost serendipitously purchased vintage crepe irons off Craigslist that led him to start cooking crepes at local art events and in his backyard for friends and family.

- Why Fuemmeler traveled to Seattle to purchase a used bus he found on eBay

- The story how Fuemmeler's newly purchased bus, broke down in Portland and ended up being featured on the local news for slowing down traffic.

- How the Fuemmeler brothers used a program called Sketchup to get a digital 3D outline of the bus before starting the conversion work to ensure the refrigerator, crepe iron, sinks, and other equipment would fit. Essentially, they built the bustaurant online before ever touching the bus.

- Some of the scrappy ways the brothers built their truck, including borrowing tools and installed their generator.

- Fuemmeler's thoughts on whether or not building a food truck from scratch is the right choice for you.

- Why Fuemmeler called the city inspectors prior to even beginning the build process

- That the Fuemmeler brothers invested about 3-months straight to build their bus

- Why you should do research on where you can and can't park in your city. Especially if you plan on operating a bustaurant. ☺

- How Fuemmeler found a niche parking at coffee shops and breweries

Resources

The Boiler Monkey Mobile Restaurant (http://www.theboilermonkey.com/)– This is the official home of The Boiler Monkey. Read more about the story of how Fuemmeler brothers got their mobile bistro.

Tumblr Account (http://boilermonkey.tumblr.com/)– In this blog, you get access to the details of the story Matt shared on the podcast. You'll find before and after photos of the bustaurant, along with images of the build process, and descriptions of the various electrical, welding, and woodwork obstacles that were encountered along the way. But after months of hard work, the Fuemmeler brothers had their dream bus.

SketchUp (http://www.sketchup.com/)– Program used to make a 3D model of the bus.

Why Food Trucks Fail

(http://foodtruckempire.com/interviews/fail/)– New blog post referenced during the podcast.

How to design your truck for food delivery speed.

Download This MP3 Interview Here:

http://foodtruckempire.libsyn.com/episode-018-interview-with-mark-s-grill-and-how-to-handle-bad-reviews

This is a new paradigm of lunch delivery food. *– Mark Hamilton reflecting on the first time he encountered a food truck.*

The guys that are making money are doing it very fast. The people that aren't are very slow. *- Mark Hamilton on food truck operations.*

In interview four, we speak with Mark Hamilton of Mark's Grill out of Memphis, Tenn. Hamilton worked in computer programming and IT for over 30 years before aborting his corporate gig and operating a different kind of program entirely: Mark's Grill. With no formal training or restaurant experience, simply a love of cooking Hamilton got to work building his truck during the evenings and weekends while still employed.

In this exclusive interview, Hamilton shares his methodology for serving fast, crave-able food and shares his secret on how to avoid the "wear out factor" that plaques so many food trucks. To solve this problem, Hamilton prescribes a mindset shift to a "more the merrier" philosophy. If you've got at least 3 – 4 food trucks parked around you, you can visit the same location multiple times while avoiding burnout from customers. By working as a group you can also attract more attention. You'll find all this advice and specific tips on increasing the work flow of your kitchen.

Stuff You'll Learn

- How Hamilton worked with his city council in

Memphis to negotiate and help educate local government about food trucks.

- Why Hamilton decided to create his own vehicle, purchased a Morgan Olson 18 foot cargo step van, gutted it, and put in a complete restaurant kitchen.

- Learn how the kitchen of Mark's Grill was designed for speed and efficiency. It's pretty intense.

- How Hamilton built a workflow for taking orders, gathering items, and getting product out the window as quickly as possible.

- Why the speed at which you can serve customers can literally make or break a food business

- How to identify a food niche in your area

- How Hamilton trains a team of four people to operate the truck

- Why you should invest a lot of time considering the layout of your mobile kitchen

- The importance of having multiple locations to park

- Why you should always work in teams of food trucks and never park alone

Resources

Mark's Grill (http://www.marksgrill.com/)– This is the official website of Mark's Grill. Check out the menu and find out where in Memphis the truck will be located next.

PART THREE

THE COST OF RUNNING A FOOD TRUCK

Food trucks are advertised as a cheap way to start a business. But if you're planning to get into the food truck business solely for the reason for low start-up costs think again. The initial investment and on-going monthly costs are significant. In this chapter, we'll outline the basic costs starting a food truck and provide a spreadsheet you can use to estimate the price of getting in the game.

Food Truck Expense Breakdown (https://docs.google.com/spreadsheet/ccc?key=0Am6SvfmhxYNsdE1VMmdTX1kxdlY5M0M3eHJ5UVBtV1E&usp=sharing) – *Download this spreadsheet and plug-in your own numbers to get an overall estimate of what it will cost to get the business up and rolling.*

The Myth

A couple reasons food trucks are considered a low-cost business is that you don't need to sign a lease for single restaurant location and can get by with few employees if you plan to manage the day-to-day operations yourself. These advantages are true, but that doesn't mean there won't be overhead.

Depending on the regulations of your city, you may be required to use a commissary. Commissary costs can run from $400 – $800 per month depending on the services that are provided and location. You'll also need to pay for insurance that can easily run from $2000 – $4000 per year depending on coverage levels and what percentage of the year you plan to operate the truck. There's also permits and business license fees that are required just like any other business. Then there's the truck.

The food truck or trailer is the biggest and most part of your investment. After all this is where you'll be spending most of your time, cooking, and it also promotes the brand and vision of your vending. You've probably read that the cost of a food truck can vary greatly. Anywhere from $15,000 – $100,000 is the range that a food truck can cost, but most fall somewhere in the middle.

Reader Warning: *Most experienced and successful long-term food truckers will tell you that opting for the cheapest vehicle and equipment isn't the way to go. The vehicle truly is the heart and sole of your business and investing in better quality equipment can help reduce repair frequency and help ensure you've got more up-time.*

Here are a few supplementary resources you can use to get a wider swath of perspectives on the costs of operating a food truck:

Are Food Truck Start Up Costs Low?

(http://thepeachedtortilla.com/food-trucks-low-
start/)– Eric Silverstein is the owner of The Peached
Tortilla, an award winning food truck in Austin, Texas.
In this article Silverstein shares his perspective on the
topic of food trailers being a low-barrier to entry
business.

Food Truck Economics

(http://blog.priceonomics.com/post/45352687467/foo
d-truck-economics) - In-depth breakdown and analysis
of the expenses of operating a food truck.
Recommended reading.

We encourage you to download the food truck cost
spreadsheet (available here:
https://docs.google.com/spreadsheet/ccc?
key=0Am6SvfmhxYNsdE1VMmdTX1kxdlY5M0M3eHJ5
UVBtV1E&usp=sharing#gid=0) to estimate how much
starting your vehicle would cost. Remember that every

city / state will have different laws and requirements so your cost will vary.

This spreadsheet is a great way to get you in the ball-park for a cost estimate.

Thank you for reading!

Good luck on building your

own mobile food unit!

foodtruckempire.com

Made in United States
Cleveland, OH
13 February 2025

14315755R00024